SPY GUIDE

SPY SPECIAL OPS

ELSIE OLSON

Abdo & Daughters
MIDDLE GRADE NONFICTION

An imprint of Abdo Publishing
abdobooks.com

ABDOBOOKS.COM

Published by Abdo Publishing, a division of ABDO, PO Box 398166, Minneapolis, Minnesota 55439.

Printed in the United States of America, North Mankato, Minnesota
052024
092024

Design: Kelly Doudna, Mighty Media, Inc.
Production: Mighty Media, Inc.
Editor: Katherine Chu
Cover Photographs: Flickr, Wikimedia Commons

Interior Photographs: Adobe Stock, pp. 58, 59; Alamy Photo, pp. 28–29; AP Images, pp. 10, 42–43, 45, 50–51, 52 (top), 61 (top left, top right); Flickr, pp. 1, 12, 18 (bottom right), 19 (top), 21; Library of Congress, p. 27; Shutterstock Images, pp. 4–5, 30, 32, 60 (top right); U.S. Air Force, pp. 19 (bottom right), 54; U.S. Department of Defense, pp. 13, 16; U.S. Marine Corps, p. 19 (middle right); U.S. Navy, pp. 14–15, 18 (middle right); Wikimedia Commons, pp. 7, 8, 9, 18 (top, middle left, bottom left), 19 (middle left, bottom left), 20, 22–23, 24, 26, 33, 34, 35, 36–37, 38, 40–41, 44, 46, 47, 48, 52 (bottom), 53, 55, 56, 60 (top left, bottom), 61 (bottom left, bottom middle, bottom right)

Design Elements: Adobe Stock

Library of Congress Control Number: 2023949221

Publisher's Cataloging-in-Publication Data

Names: Olson, Elsie, author.
Title: Spy special ops / by Elsie Olson
Description: Minneapolis, Minnesota : Abdo Publishing, 2025 | Series: Spy guide | Includes online resources and index.
Identifiers: ISBN 9781098293178 (lib. bdg.) | ISBN 9798384912446 (ebook)
Subjects: LCSH: Intelligence service--Juvenile literature. | United States. Central Intelligence Agency--Juvenile literature. | United States. National Security Agency--Juvenile literature. | United States. Federal Bureau of Investigation--Juvenile literature. | Espionage--Juvenile literature. | Spies--Juvenile literature.
Classification: DDC 327.12--dc23

CONTENTS

Before Operation Neptune Spear, the US military hadn't even acknowledged the existence of stealth helicopters.

CHAPTER 1

OPERATION NEPTUNE SPEAR

AT 1:51 P.M. ON MAY 2, 2011, A TEAM OF US TROOPS LOAD INTO two stealth Black Hawk helicopters stationed in Afghanistan. The US military has modified the helicopters with stealth technology, making them nearly impossible to detect using radar. The Black Hawks are truly incredible machines, but the troops they are carrying may be even more impressive.

The 23 men aboard the helicopters are Navy SEALs, members of one of the most elite military units in the world. An Arabic-language interpreter, a SEAL combat dog, and two backup helicopters accompany them. The Navy SEALs are one of the special operations, or special ops, forces of the US Navy. As a special ops team, these highly trained commandos complete missions that the average soldier, sailor, airman, or marine cannot. They work in small teams called units, conducting guerrilla warfare, gathering intelligence, and performing rescue missions. But this mission may be the most covert and dangerous one yet.

The 23 SEALs are members of the Navy's most highly regarded special ops team, SEAL Team Six. And they are on the most important mission of their careers, code-named Operation Neptune Spear. SEAL Team Six is flying 162 miles (261 km) toward a sprawling compound in Abbottabad, Pakistan, to find the most-wanted man in the world: terrorist leader Osama bin Laden.

A DEADLY ATTACK

The groundwork for Operation Neptune Spear began nearly a decade earlier. On September 11, 2001, a group of terrorists hijacked four US airplanes, crashing two of them into a pair of New York City skyscrapers. The third plane flew to Washington, DC, and crashed into the Pentagon, the US Department of Defense (DOD) headquarters. Passengers and crew overtook the terrorists on the fourth plane, causing it to crash in a Pennsylvania field before it could reach the terrorists' intended target, the US Capitol Building in Washington, DC.

The tragedy marked the deadliest terrorist attack on US soil. The country reeled as US leaders tried to piece together what happened. They soon learned the terrorists were members of an Islamic extremist group called al-Qaeda. And Osama bin Laden, the leader of al-Qaeda, had set the plot in motion.

In the aftermath of the attacks, US intelligence officials had one priority: to find and capture or kill bin Laden. For years, multiple intelligence organizations chased leads around the world, trying

Nearly 3,000 Americans died during the September 11 terrorist attacks.

without success to find bin Laden. Then, in late summer 2010, intelligence officials finally got a break.

A dedicated team of Central Intelligence Agency (CIA) analysts had been hunting bin Laden by interrogating prisoners, gathering intelligence from spies, and studying satellite images. Eventually, the CIA's search led them to two men known to serve as couriers for bin Laden. CIA analysts eventually tracked the men to a large compound at the end of a dead-end street in Abbottabad.

THE PACER

The fortresslike compound had many unusual features that caused CIA analysts to suspect someone important was hiding inside. Barbed wire and 12-to-18-foot (4 to 5 m) walls surrounded the building. The compound also had no electricity or phone service. The two couriers had to travel 90 miles (145 km) away just to make cell phone calls. It was clear whoever was inside wanted to remain hidden at all costs.

The CIA began 24-hour drone surveillance of the compound, hoping to learn who was inside. By studying the amount of laundry on a clothesline, analysts determined a family, containing about

The house in the compound had very few windows. The third-floor balcony was shielded by a seven-foot (2 m) privacy wall.

the same number of people as bin Laden's family, lived on the third floor. They also noticed that at roughly the same time each day, an older man went outside and walked around the building several times before returning inside. The CIA nicknamed him "the Pacer," and suspected he might be bin Laden.

The CIA determined the Pacer was the same height as bin Laden by measuring his shadow.

Because of the compound's high walls, the CIA was unable to get an image of the man's face or prove he was bin Laden. But analysts couldn't think of a more likely identity for the Pacer. In December 2010, US president Barack Obama ordered a team of CIA and DOD officials to plan a raid on the compound.

HATCHING A PLAN

For the first few months of 2011, the CIA and military leaders worked with President Obama to create a plan to break into the compound. Eventually, the team decided on a raid conducted by SEAL Team Six.

The SEALs had three weeks to prepare and practice for the mission. On the surface, it seemed simple and similar to many

To prepare, the SEALs studied a model of the compound and rehearsed the operation's steps. They wore the uniforms and carried the gear they would use on the actual mission.

missions the SEALs had done before. Land by helicopter at the compound. Breach the doors. Ascend to the third floor. Find the target. But the CIA, military officials, and the SEALs knew there was nothing simple about this plan. The stakes couldn't be higher.

BOOTS ON THE GROUND

On April 29, 2011, President Obama gave the order to raid the compound. At 3:30 p.m. on May 1, two Black Hawk helicopters landed at the compound. One crashed while landing, but there were no injuries, so the mission continued. The SEALs breached the compound, went straight to the third floor, and found the Pacer. The SEALs confirmed he was bin Laden and killed him along with four other people in the compound. The mission was a success.

Even with their target eliminated, the SEALs' work wasn't done. The compound was a treasure trove of intelligence. The SEALs gathered as much as they could for the CIA to analyze before leaving in the undamaged helicopter. A group stayed behind to destroy the crashed helicopter, ensuring the technology didn't fall into enemy hands, before escaping on a backup helicopter.

A PERFECT MODEL

Much of the planning for Operation Neptune Spear depended on a detailed model of the Abbottabad compound. Based on satellite photos and built by the National Geospatial-Intelligence Agency, the model looked as realistic and close to the original as possible. Model makers considered every detail. The sand was the same color as Pakistani sand, and every tree and animal matched the location of those at the compound. However, because of the mission's top-secret nature, the modelers had no idea what they were making. They only learned what they had built when a picture of their model appeared in the *New York Times* the day after the raid!

President Obama (*second from left*) and Vice President Joe Biden (*left*) with members of the national security team. At 3:53 p.m. on May 1, word reached Obama that bin Laden was dead.

By 5:53 p.m., the SEALs were all safely over the Pakistani border. At 11:35 p.m., President Obama addressed the nation, sharing the news that bin Laden had been killed. The next day, bin Laden was buried at sea by the US military in accordance with Islamic law.

SEAL Team Six was on the ground for less than 40 minutes, doing what seemed impossible just a year earlier. They proved they were one of the most elite special ops teams in the world. Yet, without the work of the CIA spies and analysts who provided intelligence about the compound and the people inside, the mission would not have been successful. Operation Neptune Spear used nearly every piece of spycraft available to the US government and showed why some in the intelligence community refer to Navy SEALs as "spies with flippers."

CAIRO THE DOG

The SEAL team that raided bin Laden's compound included Cairo, a Belgian Malinois combat dog. In 2008, Cairo started his training with Navy SEAL handler Will Chesney. Cairo's first deployment was in 2009. By the time of Operation Neptune Spear, he was nearing retirement. During the raid, Cairo and Chesney made sure corridors were clear and kept a curious crowd away from the compound while the SEALs recovered bin Laden's intelligence and blew up the crashed helicopter.

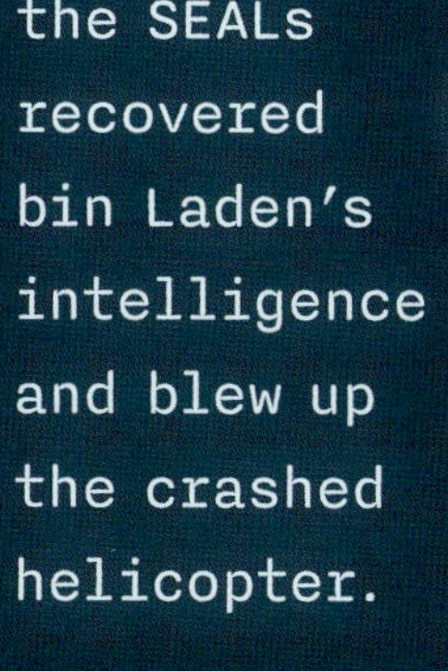

Air Force Staff Sergeant Austin West and military working dog Dak. All military working dogs must graduate from the Military Working Dog Training Program before joining regular military service.

Some special ops missions are publicized in news reports around the world. But many involve special forces working behind the scenes for months or years without public acknowledgment.

CHAPTER 2

SPECIAL OPS 101

SPECIAL OPS FORCES ARE TRAINED TO CONDUCT MILITARY activities using unconventional tactics and techniques. Their missions are often highly classified and extremely dangerous. Some missions, such as Operation Neptune Spear, are even illegal. SEAL Team Six violated international law by flying into Pakistani airspace and attacking a Pakistani residence without the Pakistan government's knowledge or permission. Still, most political, military, and intelligence officials believe the mission's result was worth the risk, since killing bin Laden likely stopped many future al-Qaeda attacks.

Special ops teams are trained to be resourceful and adaptable. They never know what missions they will go on or what problems they will have to solve. A special ops mission can take hours, days, weeks, or years. Almost any issue or problem that can't be solved through conventional means, such as the military or diplomats, can become the target of a special ops mission.

SPECIAL OPS AND SPYING

When people think of special ops, many think of the daring rescues, firefights, and raids featured in action movies. But the world of special ops is closely tied to that of espionage. Espionage is the art of stealing secret information on behalf of a government or intelligence agency, ideally without the target realizing the

Special ops teams sometimes go on reconnaissance or surveillance missions to steal top secret documents.

INTELLIGENCE SUPPORT ACTIVITY

The Intelligence Support Activity (ISA) is a highly secretive US military intelligence organization. Officially founded in 1981, the ISA provides intelligence to the military. Like the CIA, the ISA gathers human intelligence, or intelligence from spies and other human sources. It also gathers signals intelligence, or intelligence from electronic transmissions such as satellite communications, phone calls, and online correspondence. But unlike the CIA, the ISA also specializes in combat. It is so secretive that the DOD often denies knowledge of its activities.

intelligence was stolen. Special ops teams rely on this intelligence to successfully plan and execute missions, as the SEALs did in Operation Neptune Spear. But many special ops missions also actively gather intelligence.

Special ops missions are usually the result of a coordinated effort between political, military, and intelligence officials. These covert missions are handled quickly and quietly. Many special ops missions are sensitive and need to be deniable. This means the government who ordered the mission needs the ability to deny involvement if the special ops team is caught. As a result, many special ops teams dress in civilian clothes to blend into the environment they are working in. They may even grow beards or long hair, styles banned in other military units.

US SPECIAL OPERATIONS

The US military has four main branches that engage in active combat: the Navy, Army, Marine Corps, and Air Force. Each branch deploys its own special ops teams for highly sensitive missions, including counterterrorism, espionage, and rescue missions.

US SPECIAL OPERATIONS COMMAND: The command team that oversees special ops activities for all US military branches

US NAVY: Operates on, above, or below the water

SPECIAL OPERATIONS TEAMS

NAVY SEALS

- About 2,450 active-duty members
- Mission: provide immediate military relief using aspects of unconventional warfare

Navy SEALs

SPECIAL WARFARE COMBATANT-CRAFT CREWMEN

- About 600 active-duty members
- Mission: insert and extract Navy SEALs during missions

US ARMY: Operates on land, providing ground forces for the US military

Army Rangers

SPECIAL OPERATIONS TEAMS

ARMY RANGERS

- About 3,600 active-duty members
- Mission: conduct raids and assault operations behind enemy lines

DELTA FORCE

- About 1,200 active-duty members
- Mission: counterterrorism operations in foreign countries

SOAR (NIGHT STALKERS)

» About 2,700 active-duty members

» Mission: provide air support for special ops missions, specializing in nighttime operations

SPECIAL FORCES (GREEN BERETS)

» About 7,000 active-duty members

» Mission: use guerrilla warfare techniques to fight terrorists and insurgents

Green Berets

US MARINE CORPS: Operates on land and in water, providing land, sea, and air support for the US Navy

SPECIAL OPERATIONS TEAMS

MARINE CORPS SPECIAL OPERATIONS COMMAND (MARINE RAIDERS)

» About 3,000 active-duty members

» Mission: use unconventional warfare tactics for immediate missions, including counterterrorism and intelligence gathering

Marine Raiders

US AIR FORCE: Operates in the air, using airplanes and helicopters

SPECIAL OPERATIONS TEAMS

PARARESCUE

Pararescue

» Around 500 active-duty members

» Mission: parachute into hostile or hard-to-reach locations and provide medical support to injured troops

SPECIAL TACTICS

» About 2,500 active-duty members

» Mission: use airpower to provide support for ground operations

TOOLS OF THE TRADE: SPECIAL OPS EDITION

Several tools help special ops teams complete their missions. Explore the high-tech gear used by the US military!

NIGHT VISION GOGGLES

This specialized eyewear allows special ops commandos to see in the dark.

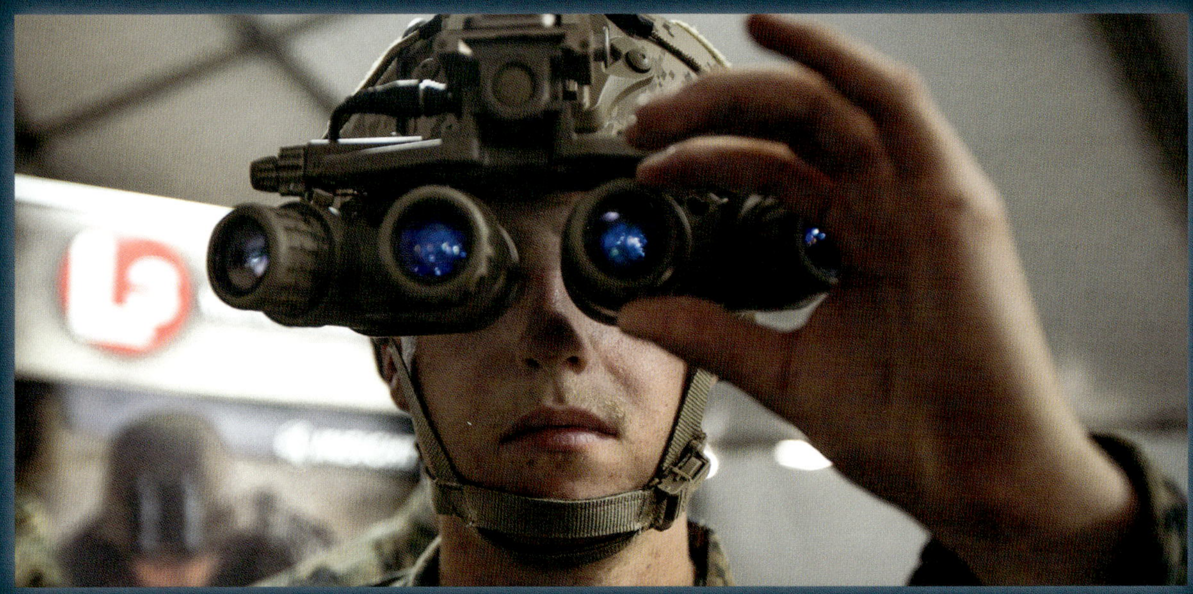

A marine tests new night optics technology during an Urban Advanced Naval Technology Exercise in 2018.

PRISM 200

This high-tech handheld device provides radar imagery of activity on another side of a wall. The Prism 200 can see up to 66 feet (20 m) through concrete, brick, and wood structures, providing valuable reconnaissance intelligence.

TEC TORCH

This small but powerful device has a flame that burns higher than 4,000 degrees Fahrenheit (2,204°C), hot enough to cut through metal, concrete, and brick. This allows special ops teams to breach walls and doors.

PARACHUTE

Special ops teams often use parachutes to access locations where helicopters can't safely land due to hostile forces or difficult terrain.

Paratroopers from the 173rd Airborne Brigade parachute into northern Italy as part of a training exercise.

CAMOUFLAGE

Special ops troops often wear camouflage to blend in with the environment they are operating in.

Soldiers often wear full-body camouflage suits, known as ghillie suits.

Ninja were typically members of lower-class Japanese society, including farmers or thieves. However, they were often trained to fight using swords and martial arts.

CHAPTER 3

EARLY SPECIAL OPS

THE HISTORY OF SPECIAL OPS GOES BACK ALMOST AS FAR as the history of human civilization itself. Around 247 BCE, Hamilcar Barca, a general in Sicily, used guerrilla tactics against his enemies. As long as there has been warfare and conflicts, politicians and military leaders have relied on special forces for the riskiest and most sensitive missions.

In the mid-1400s CE, Japan entered a period of conflict known as *Sengoku*, or "Warring States." Until the early 1600s, competing lords called *daimyo* fought one another for territory and power, making intelligence gathering and reconnaissance essential. *Daimyo* relied on special forces known as *shinobi*, or "ninja," to do their dirty work. Ninja missions included espionage, scouting, assassinations, and sabotage. Most ninja weren't loyal to a specific *daimyo*. Instead, they were mercenaries working for the highest bidder.

ROGERS' RANGERS

Many consider the first official American special forces unit to be Rogers' Rangers, a group of 600 militia frontiersmen who operated during the French and Indian War. At the time, both Great Britain and France had established colonies in North America. Conflict was inevitable as both countries competed over territory. In 1754, Britain declared war on France.

During this time, thousands of Native people already populated North America. Most fought with France against Britain. Native warriors were skilled at wilderness survival and guerrilla warfare tactics, and were experts in their terrain. This gave the French a huge advantage during the war.

Rogers (*pictured*) and his men adopted Native tactics, including wearing camouflage and performing surprise raids.

In 1755, British American captain Robert Rogers founded his own guerrilla warfare unit, Rogers' Rangers. The soldiers of Rogers' Rangers were expert woodsmen with wilderness survival skills. They valued self-sufficiency and stealth, allowing them to perform valuable reconnaissance and gain intelligence about their enemy's troop numbers, locations, and weapons.

During a battle in the winter of 1757, Rogers led a unit of 74 Rangers in a surprise attack against French forces near Ticonderoga, New York. The Rangers captured some French soldiers before French forces ambushed them. However, unlike the French, Rogers and his men were wearing snowshoes and escaped through the deep snow with few casualties. The unit was so successful that by 1759, the British had expanded the Rangers to include 12 companies.

AMERICAN RANGERS

Rogers' Rangers paved the way for future American rangers. In 1775, the American Revolution started. American colonists fought for independence from the British. During this time, a French and Indian War veteran named Thomas Knowlton became the leader of America's first intelligence unit, Knowlton's Rangers.

After a string of early American defeats, American general George Washington approached Knowlton. Washington needed an elite unit solely responsible for providing him with military intelligence. Knowlton had earned a reputation as a skilled scout during the French and Indian War, so Washington knew he was the man to lead this unit.

Knowlton recruited a group of 150 men to serve as Knowlton's Rangers. Their primary mission was to gather intelligence and perform reconnaissance. But they also took on covert direct-action missions, including sabotage and raids. Unfortunately, Knowlton was killed during a reconnaissance mission in September 1776, and the Rangers were dissolved soon after. Although Knowlton's Rangers only operated for three months, they have an important legacy as America's first military intelligence agency.

Over the next few centuries, many other governments started their own special ops units. Special ops would be especially important in the 1900s as the world entered both World War I and World War II.

Knowlton was killed during the Battle of Harlem Heights. To remember his contribution, the US Army's Military Intelligence Corps honors those who contribute significantly to military intelligence with a Knowlton Award.

« SPY HALL OF FAME »

NATHAN HALE

One of the most famous members of Knowlton's Rangers was spy Nathan Hale. In the summer of 1776, Hale volunteered for a highly dangerous espionage mission, to gather intelligence on British-controlled Long Island, New York. Washington hoped Hale's information would help the American army successfully take back control of New York City. Hale disguised himself as a Dutch schoolteacher and spent several weeks gathering information on British troops. However, on September 21, the British captured Hale trying to cross back into American territory. He was executed the next day.

Some believe Robert Rogers, who had joined the British, betrayed Hale (*center*). Many Patriots viewed Hale as a martyr, making him one of the most famous American spies in history.

A film about Operation Gunnerside was released in 1948 called *Operation Swallow: The Battle for Heavy Water*. Many men involved in the operation played themselves in the film.

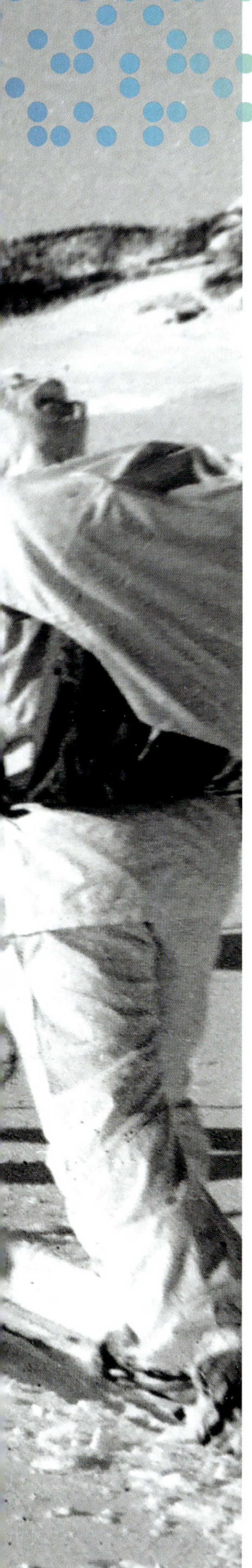

CHAPTER 4

SPIES AND SABOTAGE

IN FEBRUARY 1943, NORWEGIAN ROYAL ARMY COLONEL LEIF Tronstad handed suicide pills to six special ops soldiers in front of him. The men had recently completed a rigorous training program through the Norwegian branch of the Special Operations Executive (SOE), an elite force of guerrilla fighters, saboteurs, and spies. Now the men were about to embark on a dangerous unknown mission. Tronstad assured them that if successful, their mission would go down in history, possibly changing the course of the war.

World War II had been raging for the last four years, and Germany had occupied Norway since the summer of 1940. This caused many Norwegians, like Tronstad, to join the resistance and fight for their freedom.

Tronstad hoped his men wouldn't need the suicide pills. But the team's covert mission, code-named Operation Gunnerside, was extremely dangerous. Just three months earlier, a group of British saboteurs had attempted the same mission with the help of a small Norwegian team. They failed disastrously, with the Germans executing many of the British and leaving the small Norwegian team stranded in the mountains. The men of Operation Gunnerside didn't know why the mission was important, but knew they could be heroes to their country and much of the world if it was successful.

SABOTAGE ON SKIS

Operation Gunnerside's mission was to breach a remote German power plant in the Norwegian mountains. The only way to access

The Norwegian troopers had to sneak into the Vemork hydroelectric power plant. The plant was built into a ravine above a valley surrounded by steep mountains.

it was a single-lane suspension bridge. Barbed wire fences, land mines, and searchlights protected the plant. Once inside, the men would have to access and destroy a secret room deep in the basement.

On February 16, 1943, the six Norwegian troopers parachuted into the mountains, meeting up with the four Norwegians who had been surviving in the mountains since the failed British mission. A Norwegian spy also joined the group, bringing their numbers to 11. The winter weather was brutal, with temperatures regularly falling below zero degrees Fahrenheit (–18°C) and constant wind. The snow was so deep that the only way to travel was on cross-country skis. Luckily, the men were expert skiers who had spent months training and honing their skills.

On February 27, the team skied into the valley near the power plant, crossed a partially frozen river, and scaled the 500-foot (152 m) cliff to the plant's entrance. Because the Germans thought this route was inaccessible, there were few guards posted. The Norwegians were able to sneak past them and into the plant.

PERFECTLY PLANNED

Tronstad had spent months planning for Operation Gunnerside. Spies had provided him with maps of the plant, which Tronstad and his team had studied carefully before the mission. By the time the team breached the plant, they knew the location of every window, door, corridor, and alarm in the facility, allowing them to enter without alerting the Germans.

Germany rebuilt the power plant, but the attack had slowed their progress down so much that it was too late to affect the outcome of World War II.

The men quickly found the basement where the Germans were manufacturing heavy water, a key ingredient in developing atomic weapons. They planted timed explosives, destroying the room. Then they escaped on skis to Sweden, a country that remained neutral during the war. Operation Gunnerside's success was remarkable because no lives were lost and not a single shot was fired.

THE CHEMISTRY OF HEAVY WATER

Most water molecules contain two hydrogen atoms and one oxygen atom. However, some water molecules contain an isotope of hydrogen, called deuterium. Deuterium has twice as much mass as hydrogen, so water containing deuterium is called heavy water. Natural heavy water is very rare and hard to find. Only one water molecule in every 20 million water molecules naturally has deuterium.

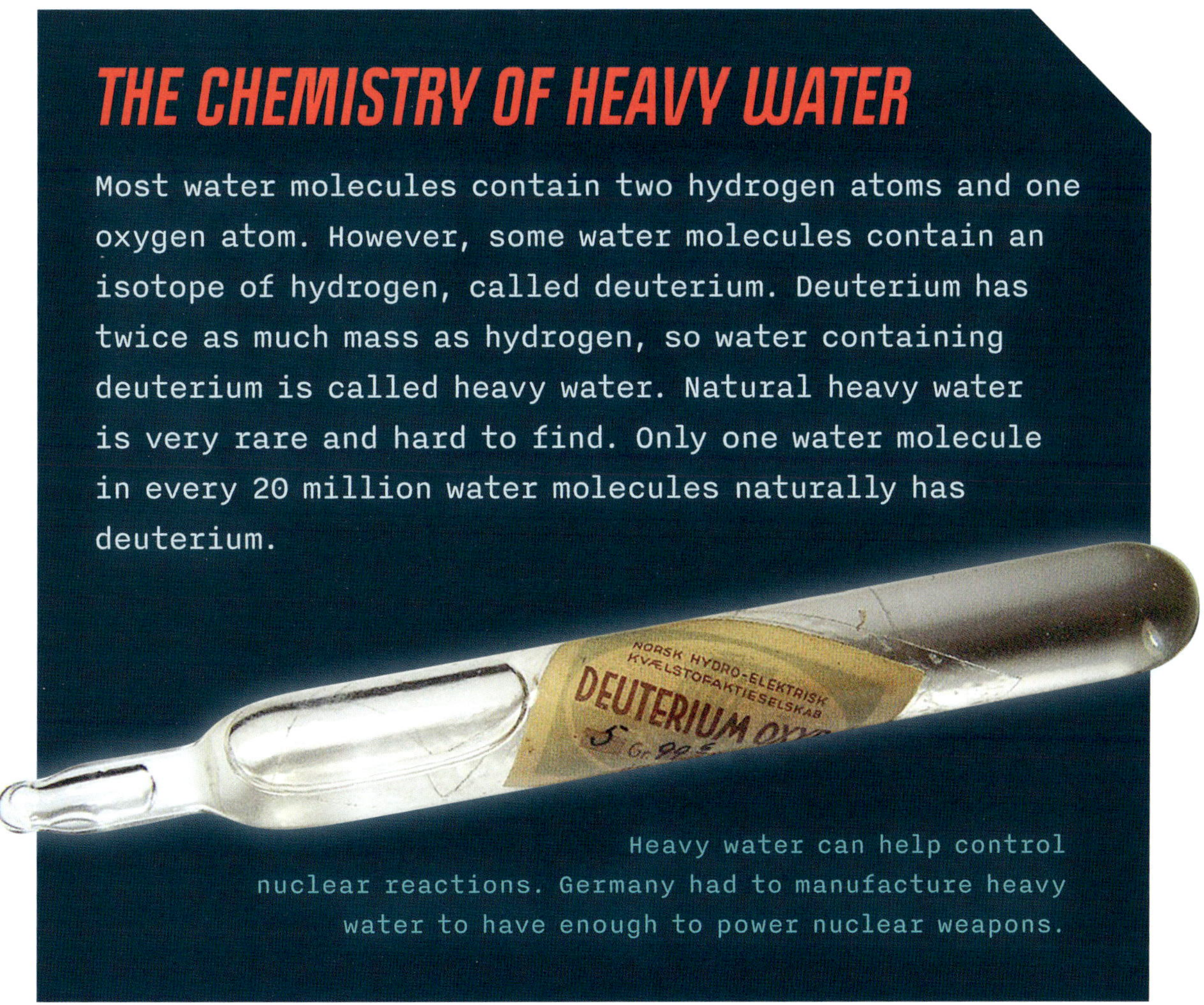

Heavy water can help control nuclear reactions. Germany had to manufacture heavy water to have enough to power nuclear weapons.

SETTING EUROPE ABLAZE

In 1940, England had set up the SOE. Its mission was to secretly gather intelligence behind enemy lines and disrupt German operations. In the words of British prime minister Winston Churchill, the SOE was to "set Europe ablaze." The Operation Gunnerside team spent months training with the SOE in the Scottish wilderness prior to their mission. They learned to survive harsh conditions and manage mental stress during nighttime training missions in the mountains.

During World War II, many SOE fighters were trained at Milton Hall in Cambridgeshire, England, before parachuting into France.

To disrupt German operations, the SOE relied on sabotage. This meant damaging or destroying military materials, such as aircraft, weapons, or other technology. Many SOE operatives worked in German-occupied countries, including France, Belgium, Greece, and Italy. This gave them access to German equipment, but made communication challenging. So, SOE operatives often had to rely on their training and wits alone when on a mission.

« SPY HALL OF FAME »

VIRGINIA HALL

In the early 1940s, the SOE recruited and trained 39 women to serve as spies in German-controlled France. The women all spoke French and were familiar enough with French culture to blend in. They trained in espionage skills, including lock picking, avoiding capture, maintaining cover, and burglary skills.

One of the most famous female SOE spies was American Virginia Hall. Hall wanted to join the Foreign Service as a diplomat but was rejected because she had a prosthetic leg due to a previous hunting accident. After World War II broke out, Hall joined the SOE. After intense training, the SOE deployed Hall to France in 1941. She spent 13 months organizing spy networks, setting up safe houses, and gathering intelligence, all while being hunted by the German military police. In 1942, Hall fled to the US. There, she joined the Office of Strategic Services.

After the war ended in 1945, US general William Donovan awarded Hall with the Distinguished Service Cross. She continued to work for the CIA until her retirement in 1966.

The USS *Halibut* rested on ski legs on the ocean floor, 400 feet (120 m) below the water's surface.

CHAPTER 5

SPECIAL INTELLIGENCE

IN THE SUMMER OF 1972, A SMALL TEAM OF US NAVY DIVERS left the relative comfort of the USS *Halibut* submarine for the icy water of the Sea of Okhotsk. If it wasn't for the warm water being constantly pumped into their dive suits, they would have frozen to death almost instantly. Using only small dive lights to pierce the darkness, the divers began walking along the ocean floor.

These men were part of a covert mission so secret and risky they didn't know its true purpose. The submarine stopped just a few miles off the coast of the Union of Soviet Socialist Republics (USSR), or Soviet Union. In 1972, during the height of the Cold War between the US and the USSR, this was a very dangerous place to be.

DIVING FOR SECRETS

The mission, code-named Operation Ivy Bells, was a collaboration between the CIA and the

US Navy. It was the idea of James Bradley Jr., the undersea warfare director for the US Office of Naval Intelligence. A few years earlier, US officials had confirmed the existence of an underwater cable attached to a Soviet naval base on the Siberian coast near the Sea of Okhotsk. It connected to a base near the USSR's border with China and North Korea.

Soviet military personnel used the cable to communicate with officials in Moscow, Russia. At the time, nearly all communication was encrypted. However, because of this cable's remote location in USSR territory, Soviet officials didn't bother encrypting messages going through it. If the US accessed the cable, officials could listen to everything the Soviets were saying. But it wouldn't be easy.

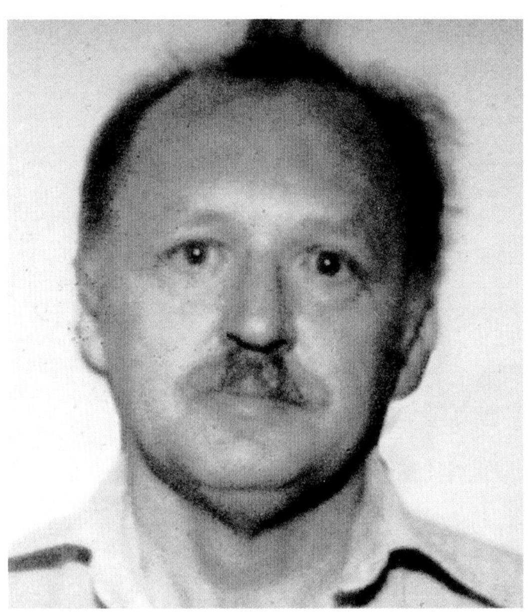

Operation Ivy Bells was successful until Ronald Pelton, an NSA veteran who became a Soviet spy, revealed the project to the USSR in 1981. The Soviets found and removed the device, ending the project.

The cable was only 5 inches (13 cm) wide. And Bradley needed to find it in more than 600,000 square miles (1,600,000 sq km) of ocean water. He remembered seeing signs on the Mississippi River when he was a child warning fishermen and other boaters not to anchor near underwater cables. Bradley correctly suspected the Soviets might use similar signs near their cable. Finding the signs led Bradley to the cable. Now, the US needed a way to access the cable's contents without the Soviets' knowledge.

Bradley worked with engineers to design a clamp that could attach to the cable without piercing it. The clamp contained tape recorders that would capture any communication going through the cable. Every few months, divers would switch out the tape recorders. If Soviets ever needed to bring the cable to the surface for repair, the clamp would automatically detach.

It took the divers hours to install the clamp, but it worked. Almost immediately, Soviet conversations flooded into the USS *Halibut*. The mission was a success! Many experts credit Operation Ivy Bells with helping to end the Cold War.

BECOMING A SPECIAL OPS COMMANDO

Joining a US special ops team isn't easy. It takes years of grueling training, and only the best of the best complete the program. To qualify for a US special ops team, you must be a US citizen who is at least 20 years old. Most special ops candidates are already members of a US military branch, but civilians can apply for some special ops teams. No matter which team you apply for, you'll need to meet physical and medical requirements and pass a series of physical, technical, and psychological exams to qualify for training. If you pass the qualification phase, you'll go through some of the toughest training imaginable. But you'll graduate a member of one of the most elite teams in the US.

THE INFORMATION GAME

During the Cold War, the US and its allies competed with the USSR for technological and military superiority. The countries never openly fought during this time. Instead, they waged secret battles using information to keep their rivals from gaining too much power. Those on both sides of the conflict worked to understand the plans and intentions of their enemy, often using special ops missions.

The intelligence industry thrived during this time, with hundreds of thousands of spies working to gather state secrets. Countries around the world established and grew intelligence agencies to manage espionage activities. The USSR had the KGB and GRU. Britain had MI6. And the US had the FBI and CIA. In addition to gathering information, these organizations performed another very important role: counterintelligence.

During the Cold War, counterintelligence was just as important as intelligence. It includes activities designed to mislead the enemy, prevent espionage, and protect national secrets. Counterintelligence officials also work to catch spies working against them and acquire knowledge or resources before their rivals can.

One of the most famous counterintelligence missions of the Cold War was Operation Paperclip. It involved a group of highly trained agents from the US Army's Counterintelligence Corps (CIC), an agency formed in 1942 to help investigate and prevent foreign intelligence threats. During Operation Paperclip, the CIC worked to bring former German Nazi scientists and engineers to the US to develop US weapons. US officials hoped this would prevent the Soviets from gaining technical superiority during the Cold War.

Not all special ops missions rely on super scientists. Some operations use old-school spycraft techniques. And one of the most famous rescue missions in US history relied on the art of disguise.

Operation Paperclip brought more than 1,500 German scientists, technicians, and engineers to the US.

The six Americans were (*from left to right*) Robert Anders, Joseph Stafford, Kathleen Stafford, Henry Lee Schatz, Cora Amburn-Lijek, and Mark Lijek.

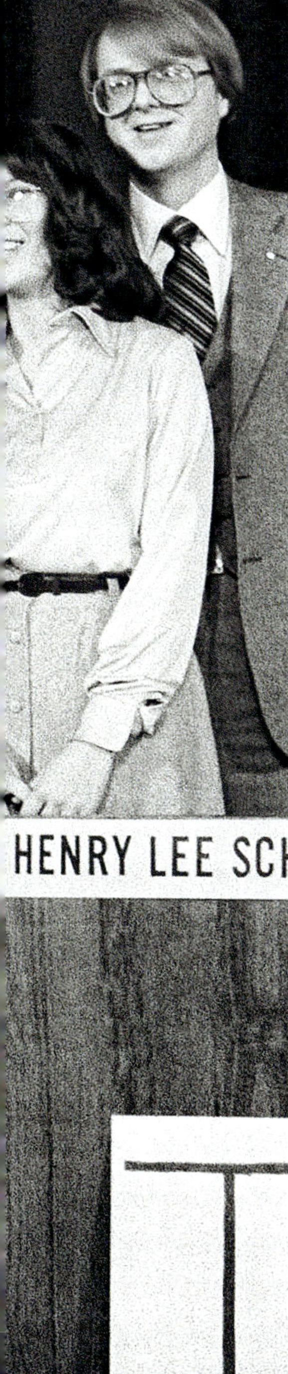

CHAPTER 6

INSERTION AND EXTRACTION

IN THE EARLY MORNING OF JANUARY 27, 1980, A SMALL Canadian film crew made its way through the Mehrabad Airport in Tehran, Iran. The group had supposedly been in the country scouting locations to shoot an upcoming science-fiction film called *Argo*. All six men and women carried Canadian passports and tickets for a 7:35 a.m. flight to Frankfurt, Germany. But first, they had to get through Iran's Revolutionary Guard security and immigration checks.

The film crew nervously handed over their identification documents, making it through security. Soon after, they were on an airplane bound for Germany. That same day, Canadian embassy officials shut down their Iranian embassy and fled the country.

These events may have seemed like a coincidence. But the real story broke a few days later. The Canadian film crew was actually comprised of six American embassy workers who had escaped a hostage situation. They spent the last few months hiding in the homes of two Canadian officials living in Iran. With the help of the Canadian government, the CIA had orchestrated an elaborate rescue plan called the Canadian Caper.

A QUIET ESCAPE

The courageous rescue of the six Americans took place during the Iranian Revolution, which lasted from 1978 to 1979. During this time, thousands of Iranian citizens overthrew their ruler, Mohammad Reza Shah Pahlavi, whom the US supported. On November 4, 1979, the revolutionaries stormed the US embassy in Iran, taking 66 American embassy workers hostage.

However, six Americans managed to escape, sheltering in the homes of Canadian diplomats Ken Taylor and John Sheardown. As time passed, it became clear that the Americans needed to escape Iran. The longer they stayed, the greater the risk to them and their Canadian protectors.

At the time of the revolution, many Iranian citizens also rejected any Western culture, which led to them storming the US embassy.

Rescue would be challenging. The US and Iran had stopped all diplomatic relations,

« SPY HALL OF FAME »

TONY MENDEZ

Tony Mendez joined the CIA in 1965 as a document forger. He went on undercover missions around the world, later joining the CIA's Office of Technical Service. This is the CIA department dedicated to creating the latest, greatest spy gadgets and disguises. Mendez's creativity and artistic skills served him well. He collaborated with Hollywood special effects and makeup artists to develop elaborate disguises. He also borrowed tricks from magicians to make his disguises even better. Mendez was well known for his ability to blend in with the local culture wherever he traveled.

Tony Mendez (*right*) with his wife, Jonna Mendez. Both served as the CIA's master of disguise at different times, overseeing the development of new disguises for the CIA's field agents.

which meant Americans couldn't enter or leave the country. And a military rescue could prove deadly for the Americans and the Canadians. So the US would have to extract the six men and women quietly, as passengers on commercial flights.

To make matters worse, the Iranian revolutionaries had captured the three CIA field agents who were already in Iran. To successfully rescue the six Americans, the CIA would first need to insert new agents into Iran. Luckily, they knew the perfect man for this logistical nightmare. The agency called in CIA veteran Tony Mendez, an expert in disguises, forging documents, and exfiltration, the art of covertly inserting and extracting people from hostile areas. Working with the Canadians, Mendez began orchestrating an elaborate plan.

ARGO

Posing as Irish film producer Kevin Costa Harkins, Mendez set up a fake film production company called Studio Six Productions in Los Angeles,

Mendez used a script from a previously canceled science-fiction movie. He published stories in American magazines about the film, which he renamed *Argo*, convincing the Iranian government of its authenticity.

California. The studio was complete with business cards and phone lines. To make the deception more believable, Mendez enlisted the help of real Hollywood special effects and makeup artists. Mendez and his team also developed cover stories for all six Americans, who would pose as Harkins's Canadian film crew.

US president Jimmy Carter (*right*) congratulates Mendez after the successful mission.

On January 26, Mendez, disguised as Harkins, flew into Iran. He had sent exfiltration supplies ahead to the Canadian embassy, including items supporting the Americans' cover, such as movie cameras and receipts from Canadian restaurants. Mendez also brought important documents to support the cover stories, including Canadian passports, visas, driver's licenses, and health cards. He helped the Americans put on disguises and memorize their cover stories. They didn't have much time. The "film crew" was scheduled to fly out of Iran the following day.

On January 27, Studio Six received a phone call on a secret line only used by the CIA. "It's over," a voice said. "They're out." Mendez had pulled off one of the most daring rescues in CIA history. Studio Six quietly closed its doors soon after.

Bravo Company, part of the 3rd Battalion of the 75th Ranger Regiment deployed in Somalia in 1993

GETTING IN AND OUT

Exfiltration, also known as infiltration and extraction, includes some of the most important special ops missions, which involve removing people from hostile areas or situations. These operations usually occur when military or civilian personnel are in immediate danger. They must be planned and executed quickly with little room for error. But not all insertions and extractions are done as quietly as the Canadian Caper.

In October 1993, a group of US Army Rangers and Delta Force were deployed into Mogadishu, Somalia, to protect United Nations shipments of food and aid, which were being stolen by local Somali warlords. The mission was to capture or kill the leading

OPERATION EAGLE CLAW

While Mendez was working to rescue the six Americans, US officials also worked to save the Americans captured when the Iranians first stormed the embassy. When US president Jimmy Carter approved a rescue plan called Operation Eagle Claw in April 1980, the Iranians still held 53 Americans hostage. The operation began on April 27. It involved every branch of the US military. However, during the mission, the rescue helicopters flew into a dangerous sandstorm known as a haboob. One of them crashed, and Carter called off the mission. Iran later released the hostages on January 20, 1981, following diplomatic negotiations.

warlord. Some of the special forces arrived in heavily armored vehicles. Others came in Black Hawk helicopters, two of which were immediately shot down, trapping the crews in the city. The firefight that followed lasted days, killing 19 Americans and around 700 to 1,500 Somalis.

The event became known as the Battle of Mogadishu, part of an effort by the US to fight terrorism in North Africa and the Middle East that lasted well into the 2000s. And it would give rise to some of the most famous special ops missions in US history.

Hussein hid in a hole just large enough to fit one person.

CHAPTER 7

DIRECT ACTION AND THE FUTURE OF ESPIONAGE

THE SUN HAD ALREADY SET ON DECEMBER 13, 2003, WHEN a team of elite US commandos converged on a muddy orange grove near the small town of Tikrīt, Iraq. The commandos were part of Task Force 121, a secret multiservice special ops force including members of Delta Force, Navy SEALs, Army Rangers, conventional military forces, and CIA officers. The unit's primary mission was to capture high-value targets (HVTs) after the March 2003 US invasion of Iraq. They were hunting the man at the top of their most-wanted list, code-named HVT number one.

The commandos first cut the power in the village, concealing their activities under the cover of darkness. Then they searched a run-down shack near the orchard, finding evidence that someone was living there but no sign of their

A US commando stands inside the hole where Hussein was found.

target. However, near the back of the orchard, they noticed a carpet placed beneath a date palm tree. Under the carpet was a foam cover coated with dirt.

Commandos lifted the cover, revealing a disheveled-looking bearded man with his hands in the air in surrender. As commandos pulled him out of the hole, he said, "I am Saddam Hussein. I am the president of Iraq, and I am willing to negotiate." Task Force 121 had found and captured their target, former Iraqi dictator and war criminal Saddam Hussein.

FIND, FIX, AND FINISH

The search for Hussein, code-named Operation Red Dawn, took 8 months, about 600 troops, and 300 interrogations. The US military relied on a special ops tactic for their hunt known as find, fix, and finish. Find, fix, and finish is a key strategy for US direct action missions.

Hickey led the hunt, which involved months of detective work.

It was also used during the bin Laden compound raid. Direct action missions involve short-duration strikes and small-scale offensive actions, including sabotage, recovery missions, or capture of HVTs.

To capture Hussein, US officials first had to find him. Throughout the summer of 2003, teams of interrogators and CIA agents, led by Colonel James B. Hickey, questioned Iraqis living in and near Hussein's hometown of Tikrīt. The Iraqis gave the team valuable intelligence about Hussein and his family. Hickey narrowed his search down to five families in the Tikrīt area who were closest to Hussein and might be hiding him.

By December 13, Hickey had narrowed Task Force 121's search to two farmhouses and an underground cellar near Tikrīt. Commando raids of the two farmhouses were unsuccessful, but interrogating the farmers led them to Hussein's hiding spot.

Hussein was handed over to the new Iraqi government, where he stood trial and was executed in 2006.

Task Force 121 was ready to finish the mission. They had orders to capture Hussein alive if possible, but they were also heavily armed and prepared for a firefight. A team of about 24 special ops commandos searched for Hussein while 52 soldiers secured the surrounding area. Minutes later, Hussein surrendered and was taken into US custody.

THE FUTURE OF SPECIAL OPS

For most of military history, special ops relied on the men and women who undertook dangerous and covert missions. But with the rise of technology, the future of special ops may look very different. New technology such as drones, hypersonics, artificial intelligence (AI), and quantum computers are rewriting the rules of special ops.

Intelligence organizations have used surveillance drones since the 1960s. They are powerful reconnaissance tools that help special ops teams prepare for missions. But modern drones now have

The US Air Force designed the X-51A Waverider, an experimental hypersonic aircraft, in 2010.

the power to disrupt enemy communications, sabotage equipment, and take out targets. The US Navy is even working to develop undersea drones called Orcas.

The US and China are both working independently to develop a new series of hypersonics, or hypersonic weapons, that can travel five times faster than the speed of sound. These devices are so fast that they can't be detected or stopped by current missile defense equipment, making them deadlier than the best-trained special ops team.

ROBOT VS. ROBOT?

Modern digital technologies are quickly changing. The rise in quantum computing may lead to computers that are more than 100 million times faster than standard computers. Quantum computing, coupled

DARPA

The Defense Advanced Research Projects Agency (DARPA) leads military technology development for the US. Since the Cold War, DARPA has taken on technology challenges that seem impossible.

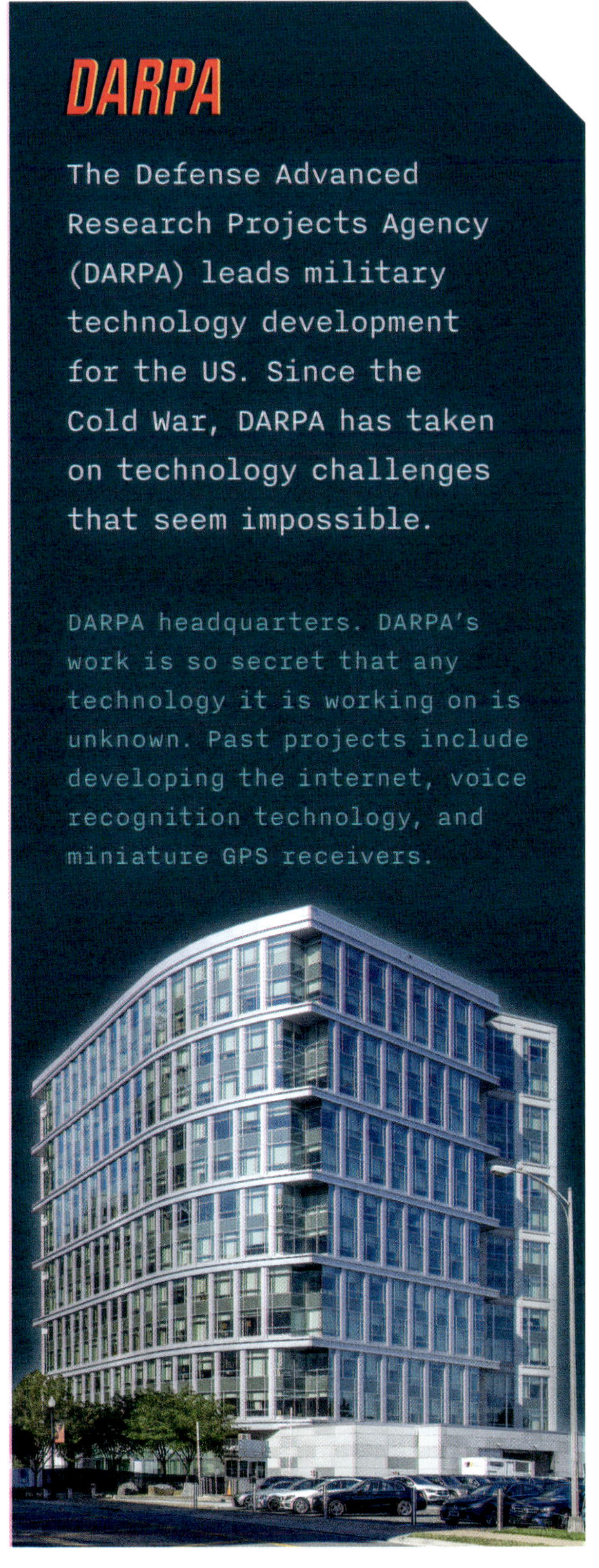

DARPA headquarters. DARPA's work is so secret that any technology it is working on is unknown. Past projects include developing the internet, voice recognition technology, and miniature GPS receivers.

In 2012, DARPA released the Legged Squad Support System, a robot that could carry more than 400 pounds (181 kg), charge electrical devices, and traverse rugged terrain.

with the rise of AI, is expected to change the face of special ops. As AI grows more powerful, future drones and other robotics technology could even plan and execute special ops missions with minimal involvement of or risk to human soldiers. Some experts predict a future where teams of robots will battle one another.

While futuristic robotic armies may spare human lives, many experts have ethical concerns about involving AI in special ops missions. Tech experts are especially concerned about giving AI autonomy over the use of deadly force during military operations. This is because AI methods are not as accurate as humans for these kinds of tasks.

This changing technology and its risks are just some of the issues special ops teams and their leaders need to consider as they move toward the future. However, no matter what new technology and techniques they use, special ops teams will continue to put their lives on the line. These brave men and women will take on risky secret missions to make the world a safer place.

UAV OR UFO?

In 2022, the Pentagon issued a report covering more than 500 unidentified flying object (UFO) sightings investigated by military and intelligence officials. Members of the US Navy and Air Force made most of the reports. The Pentagon was able to identify 366 of the UFOs. Most turned out to be unmanned aerial vehicles (UAVs) such as drones or weather balloons. However, 171 sightings did not have a known cause. Many of these UFOs seemed to use technology unknown to the US military. Many experts suspected they were foreign UAVs sent to spy on the US. But other experts wondered if some of these UFOs could be alien technology from a faraway planet.

SO YOU WANT TO BE A SPY?

Spies can be anywhere and everywhere. Your choir director, relative, or neighbor could be a spy! But being a spy who can take on the most dangerous special ops missions isn't easy. Do you have what it takes to be part of a special ops team? Complete the missions below to find out!

MISSION 1
EXPLORE INFILTRATION AND EXTRACTION

Practice the art of infiltration by attempting to insert a stuffed animal into a busy room. Choose a time when your family or friends are gathered together. See if you can covertly sneak the stuffed animal into the room without anyone noticing. Next, see if you can remove an object from the room without anyone noticing. To make the mission more challenging, choose a big object, such as a table lamp or picture frame.

MISSION 2
BUILD A SHELTER

Special ops commandos often need to be completely self-reliant when on missions. They may have little or no communication with the outside world and need to be ready to improvise at a moment's notice. Practice your survival skills by building an outdoor shelter.

Consider the materials you have to work with. If you live near a wooded park, you may have sticks and leaves. If you live in a cold area, you may have snow and ice. If you live near a beach, you may have access to driftwood and tall grass. Determine which materials will make up the base and frame of your shelter. Then weatherproof it as best you can with any additional materials you find.

MISSION 3
CREATE CAMO

Because of the covert nature of special ops missions, commandos often wear camouflage, or camo, to blend in with their surroundings. Design your own camo outfit to help you blend in with your environment. Pick clothing with colors that match the environment you are trying to blend into. Conceal any features, such as hair or skin, that might make you stand out. Now put your camo to the test. Choose a hiding spot and challenge a friend or family member to find you!

TIMELINE

Ninja become active in Japan.
1400s CE

1754–1763
The French and Indian War

1755
British American captain Robert Rogers founds a guerrilla warfare unit known as Rogers' Rangers.

The American Revolutionary War
1775–1783

Thomas Knowlton establishes a military intelligence unit known as Knowlton's Rangers.
1776

1914–1918
World War I

1939–1945
World War II

1940
England sets up an elite force of guerrilla fighters, saboteurs, and spies called the SOE.

A small team of Norwegian commandos on skis bombs a German heavy water plant in a mission known as Operation Gunnerside.
1943

1945
CIC agents begin Operation Paperclip to bring former German Nazi scientists and engineers to the US.

The Cold War
1947–1991

Six Americans disguised as a Canadian film crew successfully escape Iran thanks to a plot known as the Canadian Caper.
1980

US Task Force 121 captures Iraqi dictator Saddam Hussein.
2003

1972
Navy divers tap a Soviet underwater communication cable in a mission called Operation Ivy Bells.

1993
A group of US special ops troops are trapped in Somalia during a mission that becomes known as the Battle of Mogadishu.

2011
US Navy SEAL Team Six raids terrorist Osama bin Laden's compound in Operation Neptune Spear.

GLOSSARY

assassination–the murder of a very important person, usually for political reasons.

classified–kept from the public in order to protect national security.

commando–a military unit or member of a military unit trained for surprise raids.

counterterrorism–efforts and strategies to fight or prevent terrorism.

courier–a messenger, especially in secretive, military, or diplomatic roles.

deploy–to spread out and organize in a battle formation.

encrypt–to convert information or data into a cipher or code to prevent unauthorized access.

espionage–the secret gathering of information on others.

frontiersmen–people living in a region that forms the edge of the settled part of a country.

guerrilla warfare–fighting that uses sudden, small, surprise attacks against enemies. A guerrilla is a person, usually a member of an independent unit, who uses guerrilla warfare.

infiltrate–to enter a place secretly and without permission.

insurgent–someone who fights or revolts against a government.

interrogate–to question formally and thoroughly.

isotope–one of two or more atoms of the same element that have a different number of neutrons.

negotiate–to work out an agreement about the terms of something.

prosthetic–of, relating to, or being an artificial device that replaces a part of the body.

quantum computer–a computer that makes use of the quantum states of subatomic particles to store information.

reconnaissance–military observation of the enemy.

sabotage—to harm an enemy nation's defenses by damaging or destroying something on purpose. A saboteur is someone who sabotages an enemy nation.

spycraft—the skills and techniques employed by spies.

state secret—a piece of information kept secret by the government.

surveillance—close observation of someone or something.

terrain—an area of land or the physical features of an area of land.

terrorist—a person who uses violence to threaten people or governments.

ONLINE RESOURCES

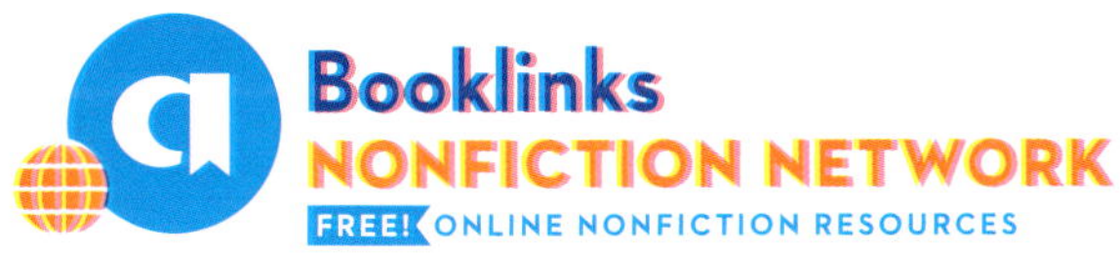

To learn more about spy special ops, please visit **abdobooklinks.com** or scan this QR code. These links are routinely monitored and updated to provide the most current information available.

INDEX